# SING NOW!

## Overcome Your Fear of Performing with Practical Advice and Exercises

By:
Bo Morgan
&
Cynthia Riess

Text Copyright © Lightbulb Publishing

All rights reserved. No part of this guide may be reproduced in any form without permission in writing from the publisher except in the case of brief quotations embodied in critical articles or reviews.

**Legal & Disclaimer**

The information contained in this book and its contents is not designed to replace or take the place of any form of medical or professional advice; and is not meant to replace the need for independent medical, financial, legal or other professional advice or services, as may be required. The content and information in this book has been provided for educational and entertainment purposes only.

The content and information contained in this book has been compiled from sources deemed reliable, and it is accurate to the best of the Author's knowledge, information, and belief. However, the Author cannot guarantee its accuracy and validity and cannot be held liable for any errors and/or omissions. Further, changes are periodically made to this book as and when needed. Where appropriate and/or necessary, you must consult a professional (including but not limited to your doctor, attorney, financial advisor or such other professional advisor) before using any of the suggested remedies, techniques, or information in this book.

Upon using the contents and information contained in this book, you agree to hold harmless the Author from and against any damages, costs, and expenses, including any legal fees potentially resulting from the application of any of the information provided by this book. This disclaimer applies to any loss, damages or injury caused by the use and application, whether directly or indirectly, of any advice or information presented, whether for breach of contract, tort, negligence, personal injury, criminal intent, or under any other cause of action.

You agree to accept all risks of using the information presented in this book.

You agree that by continuing to read this book, where appropriate and/or necessary, you shall consult a professional (including but not limited to your doctor, attorney, or financial advisor or such other advisor as needed) before using any of the suggested remedies, techniques, or information in this book.

# Table of Contents

**Chapter 1:** Introduction: About Me..................................................1

**Chapter 2:** About You: Your Kind of Music ...............................5

**Chapter 3:** Vocal Teachers: My Advice......................................9

**Chapter 4a:** A Basic Framework for Practicing.....................29

**Chapter 4b:** Simple Exercises and Tips on Posture & Breathing........35

**Chapter 5:** Respecting All Music................................................43

**Chapter 6:** Singing in a Recording Studio...............................49

**Chapter 7:** Stage Etiquette: Being Professional to All the Players (Even If You Don't Get Along)..................................57

**Chapter 8:** Why It Hurts You to Criticize Others....................59

**Chapter 9:** Dealing with Stage Fright........................................67

**Chapter 10:** Microphone Types and Technique ....................73

**Chapter 11:** Basic Movement on Stage...................................79

**Chapter 12:** Singer's Rituals and Secrets to Preserving Your Voice....81

**Chapter 13:** Advice from My Mom: Don't Feel Sorry For Yourself...87

**Chapter 14:** Next Steps................................................................91

**Chapter 15:** Conclusion ...............................................................97

# Chapter 1
# Introduction: About Me

Thank you for purchasing this book. You may find it quite a bit different from other singing books, courses, and information available out there.

## What Do I Have to Offer You?

I've been a professional singer (doing paid singing jobs or "gigs") since I was 14 years old. I am mostly self-taught and although I've trained with many coaches and teachers both privately and in academic environments, I did not receive much training until I had already worked professionally as a singer. I have quite a bit of professional experience in the field and a somewhat unique perspective which I feel is worth sharing.

Everything in this book is meant to help you get performance-ready as quickly as possible. I don't want to waste your time. I want to give it to you straight.

You may find that this information runs counter to a lot of other information traditionally available. I want to stress that I mean no disrespect to any teachers or institutions. I only intend to present other avenues of opportunity that lie just beyond view. There are quick and easy steps for those who seek the way. There is no reason anyone cannot get up on a stage and express themselves through music.

Thanks to singing, I have had the pleasure of working and living in many fantastic countries like Japan, Korea, and Taiwan, touring exciting locales such as the Bahamas, Mexico, Hong Kong, and Jamaica, while most of the time living and working in five-star hotel venues and on cruise ships.

I have sung professionally in various cities in the United States and some of the biggest festivals and venues in Canada. Usually, these singing jobs have required me to sing six nights a week, at least three to four sets per night, or in some cases five to seven sets per night, as was expected of us while working at one of the most well-known casinos in Las Vegas.

In addition to tons of live performing in the U.S., Canada, overseas, and at sea, I've also recorded with various musicians and producers. I currently run my own audio company with my husband and work as a professional composer and sound designer.

I've composed music for video games (some of which were used in public schools) and done film and animation. My music has been in advertisements and been used by CNN. I've composed and produced pieces for children's audio books, and much more.

The experiences I will share with you in this book have led me to a life of my own design, given me a way to be paid for my talents and efforts, and granted me rich musical experiences. All of these things have contributed to my ongoing education and continue to lend themselves well to what I do now – composing!

## Why Is This Relevant?

My experience has taught me how to preserve and use my voice under extreme conditions over a long period of time. I have never missed a performance due to losing my voice.

Let me repeat. Having worked extended contracts, six nights a week, for six months to two years, my voice has always held up through the job. That's a lot of singing!

Additionally, I was examined by an ear, nose, and throat doctor who looked at my vocal cords and said that he had a hard time believing that I had been singing professionally for so long. He could hardly see any signs of wear and tear or abuse of my vocal cords. He almost accused me of lying! However, I know the truth, and so do a lot of musicians who worked with me and were glad that their pay was never threatened because of the "girl singer's" voice giving out.

Anyone I worked for, or with, could always depend on my voice getting us through. I came to be known as a "secret weapon," an "ace in the hole," and a "sure thing." I was a "heavy-duty" singer who could "kick ass," and those words came from musicians I worked with, not myself! I humbly appreciate those accolades.

More about me later, let's talk about you!

# Chapter 2
# About You: Your Kind of Music

It's helpful to have an idea of what kind of singing you want to do. Usually, there is a song or genre that motivates us to sing. Think of the kind of music career that most appeals to you. What does it look like?

If you want to learn to sing, one of the most important things to consider is what kind of singing you will be doing and what your venue or stage will be.

As I mention in other areas of this book, stage singing, say for a musical theatre production, is different from singing on a stage with a band, in pop music, or in a studio setting.

Do you see yourself as a recording artist? Would you like to join a band? Perhaps you like theatre music or amazing vocalists, or maybe you prefer hip-hop and rap.

Wherever your musical love lies, it's good to respect all music and all people. I find something to appreciate in every genre, even though I may not love all of it. I love pop music and pop stars and I respect what it takes to become successful in their field. I do not believe any music deserves more respect than any other type of music.

**My Experience as a Vocal Coach**

During my time working as a vocal and beginner's guitar coach, I learned a few things from my awesome students about why some people are uncomfortable singing and performing.

In my experience, the biggest block to gaining the confidence to sing professionally is the **mindset** required, NOT the training or vocal talent.

*"You've got to believe in yourself. It really is true, because that's one thing about the Beatles... Man, we believed in ourselves! We knew we were good!"*

- Paul McCartney, pop legend

In this book, I will show you the basic exercises I have shared with my students and do myself before each of my professional singing jobs (usually in my car on the way to the gig). These simple exercises will help anyone loosen up their vocal cords. I don't rely on a lot of exercises, so they will not be the focus of this book. Most of what I will share is related to psychology.

I want to stress that this book is not written from an academic perspective. Though I have received extensive training from reputable and accredited teachers, colleges, and learning institutions, I do not suggest that any of them can help you any more than you can probably help yourself. While I have benefited from formal training, my most effective training came from learning as I went.

Disclaimer: If you want to learn any kind of technical training, such as singing opera, this book, while it may be informative, cannot take the place of specialized training. You can injure yourself and hurt your voice if you are continually screaming or abusing it. The techniques involved in some areas such as operatic singing are beyond my scope of expertise and I recommend that you visit a specialized vocal teacher.

## Let's Get You on Stage!

Let's say you have decided to sing, or someone has entered you into a contest, or you need to sing for a church, work, or school event. Here's how to get started!

1. Go over the simple vocal exercises anyone can do in any range. Do these for at least 10 minutes, but no longer than 15 or 20 minutes. As I mentioned above, I don't much care for vocal exercises, and I won't put you through more than I feel is necessary.

2. Have your song picked out. I highly recommend buying one or more backing tracks from one of the many backing track and karaoke providers online. If you know a musician, possibly a piano or keyboard player, you can ask them for help.

   Of course, you will probably need to pay them. Musicians are often expected to do things for free, but you would never ask someone to fix your plumbing or change the oil in your car as a favor, would you?

   For now, to keep the control in your hands, try working with backing tracks or karaoke. Background music can usually be purchased in higher or lower keys than the original artist's version, so you don't need Mariah Carey's range to sing one of her songs!

3. Practice that song every day. Sing through it at least three times. Record it, play it back, and then work on the parts you feel could be better. Once you have perfected that song, pick up another song and work on it in the same way. Once you have a few songs well rehearsed, sing them all in a row with your backing tracks without stopping for more than a few minutes between songs if possible.

Doing this will improve your ability to get up on stage and deliver quality performances. If you can afford a teacher, that's great, but if you cannot afford one or just don't want one, this is a valid way to improve your singing. It is also the quickest way to "quantum leap" your way into performance mode in the shortest time possible.

Learning how to sing or gaining proficiency in vocal ability does not mean that you can sing any song perfectly at any time. Not even the most talented singers in the world perform songs they've never rehearsed before. Any material you plan to perform needs its own attention and rehearsal time. This is how you begin.

*"People think I'm disciplined. It's not discipline, it is devotion. There is a great difference."*

- Luciano Pavarotti, opera icon

# Chapter 3
# Vocal Teachers: My Advice

There is no shortage of teachers in every town, school, or university who can train you in a controlled environment, using books and information that they learned in their studies.

While I attended classes, the bulk of my music education and experience came from on-the-job training. If you aspire to become, say, a university professor of music, you may need a music degree. I have coached vocal students at a few music schools because I was invited to by the heads of those schools. I never set out to become a singing teacher. Although I enjoyed the time I had with my students, I do not currently accept or seek students and most of my time is spent composing music and creating products from my studio, like this book!

## My Earliest Experiences

I did not grow up with a lot of my parents' money to spend on lessons. I had to find out how to get training without paying a lot of money. My mom said that if I wanted lessons I could have them, but it seemed like a larger-than-comfortable expense for my single mother who had no financial help from anyone. I was a latchkey kid by the age of eight or nine, and I loved singing. I learned as much as I could about it and took it seriously from a young age.

Around that time, I heard on TV that if you are diligent and you work on your craft every day, you can become good at it, even without a proper teacher.

Every day when I got home from school, I put on my mother's Barbra Streisand, Frank Sinatra, and Nancy Wilson recordings. I listened closely to recordings from the TV show Soul Train. I absorbed classic country stars like Glen Campbell and Patsy Cline and great Broadway show tunes like those sung by Jennifer Holliday in Dreamgirls. I sang along with those recordings for hours every day.

## Be Careful

This can be dangerous if you start by trying to copy Mariah Carey's vocal bells. Consistently singing out of your range can hurt your voice. However, by singing along with my mom's music collection, I was able to gain a lot of insight just by listening and paying attention to these recordings. This may sound silly, but you can learn a lot by listening carefully to the recordings of the best in the business, and that's exactly who those artists are and were.

> *"I remember singing around the house to records that were playing. All kinds of music. And the great James Cleveland was often in our house, and I grew up with this sound as well."*
>
> - Aretha Franklin, the queen of soul

One of the most important things I learned from listening closely and practicing along with these singers' recordings was breathing. I came to know the phrasing, timing, and technique employed by the best of the best.

## School Days

My elementary school had a music program which all children participated in. I was given a wonderful instrument called the autoharp. Though it perplexed me, I loved my autoharp and looked forward to my special time with it. After my teacher heard my singing voice, she declared that I would be in the singing group instead. I was bummed to lose the autoharp, but she was a great teacher and I was delighted that she thought I had a good voice.

## Confused by Music

It would not be until much later that I would understand how to play an instrument. Despite trying for many years, I couldn't understand the on-paper concepts of how music worked. I had a guitar which I could not understand how to play. I took piano and theory lessons in school but could not follow along. Maybe it would have been called ADD if they had been diagnosing it when I was in school.

Much later I would learn to play many instruments. Now, I produce music that I write and perform. I control it all. I've composed music for video games, advertisements, film, animation, and more. I started out as a singer who worked professionally and then did what many singers do and explored other realms of professional music.

This is miraculous to me because I had so much trouble learning how to understand written music and how to play instruments that getting to where I am now seemed impossible!

## A Positive and Nurturing Environment

Although my mother loved me and provided a secure and stable environment, I did not have money for special classes or lessons. Despite that, I taught myself how to play the guitar, keyboard, trumpet, harmonica, percussion instruments, and more.

None of that involved reading music. Even though music was hard for me to learn and I had to dedicate myself to learning an instrument, those things did eventually happen for me in more fulfilling ways than I could have ever imagined. However, if I could have better understood how to write my own music, or if I had learned that autoharp earlier in my elementary school days, I might have missed out on all the great experiences I had using my first instrument - my voice. Using my voice has allowed me to get paid to sing and travel to amazing places that I may have never seen otherwise.

## Look Around for Opportunities

I want the biggest takeaway from this book to be this: You have the power to express yourself through music, no matter what anyone says! You might not understand music or singing, you might think you can't do it, or maybe others have told you that they don't like your voice. WHATEVER the opposition, **nothing** else matters except your desire to express yourself through music!

Though we don't know each other, I am your friend. I believe in you. But you have to believe in yourself!

> *"Turn off any self-talk that tells you that you are destined to live a small life. You're not."*
>
> -Loral Langemeier, motivational speaker

A large part of this book is about the psychological mindset needed to sing confidently in front of others or even alone in a studio situation. There are different techniques for different types of singing and although this book does not teach all of them, I will take you through some of the differences between types of singing.

## They Must Be Born with It

I recently saw the sister of Miley Cyrus and daughter of Billy Ray Cyrus, Noah Cyrus talking about the exercises that her vocal teacher has taught her. Now the Cyrus' ain't no strangers to singing. Talent may run in the family, but consider this: They may have more confidence than the average person because they are the offspring of a popular and successful musician. This can give someone who is not from such a musical family the idea that "talent" or "ability" is out of our hands and only bestowed upon the children of talented musicians.

*Billy Ray Cyrus and Miley Cyrus*

How would we know if their musical ability was genetic or if the constant suggestions of family, friends, and fans of their famous dad lead them to assume that they were talented?

How would you know the difference between talent that was your own and talent that was passed down to you? I don't think you can ever know that. Psychologically, this can have a huge impact on how you see yourself and your chances of success.

This is not meant to suggest that Miley, Noah, and other children of celebrities are not talented on their own, only that they may have been influenced to develop their abilities by the suggestions and expectations in their environments.

# Vocal Teachers: My Advice

I love Mariah Carey; her voice is heavenly. I believe she would have been a huge success even if she had not grown up with a professional singer for a mother, but she did, so for Mariah, the idea that it was *possible* for a person to sing professionally was already there.

*Mariah Carey performing at President Obama's inauguration*

Compare this privileged situation to the kind of response many families with no musical professionals give to those seeking to sing or perform as a vocation.

They might be met with negativity, anger, ridicule, or disbelief. Rarely do you hear stories of acceptance, support, and encouragement. Having a negative environment can be a huge hurdle to overcome. What's your environment like?

By the way, I think Miley Cyrus is very talented and she knows the value of publicity. She once stated in an interview that she had been "twerking" and acting outrageous because no one was paying attention to her new album. This is a person with a famous father, a beautiful face, and a fantastic singing voice. Yet, she still had to resort to twerking for attention.

Did she get it? You tell me!

You too can find valuable opportunities which may come at no cost or low cost to you. There is no shortage of teachers for anything you want to learn. You can take private lessons from an individual or take classes at your local community college. You can take full courses in music programs designed to teach you how to perform or you can take lessons focusing on the technicalities of music. I have done all of these.

However, none of those are the same as performing outside of a controlled environment. Like you are doing now, you will probably not be singing, but reading. You will not be performing, but listening to a teacher's lecture.

Similarly, doing vocal exercises daily, while useful, **is not performing**.

I took years of classes, courses, lessons, and various forays into academic learning; most of it did not include much live performing.

What did I learn?

Each teacher has their own "program." Those programs typically consist of a lot of specific, ongoing vocal exercises.

While vocal exercises are useful, my voice never improved any more from anyone's exercises than it did from simply singing along to music when I was young.

Many teachers would disagree with this, but I feel it's worthwhile to say. Not many music teachers or vocal coaches have as much professional performing and recording experience as I do. I apologize to any vocal coaches or music teachers who take exception to this. I respect you and your work, but it is not the *only way*.

Was my training valuable? It sure was!

Many of the things I've carried to this day have come from those early years of trying to find out if there was more to learn about singing. However, it cannot replace what I learned from live performing experiences, most of which I found on my own.

## Find a Reason and a Place to Perform

I highly suggest singing in public at the first good opportunity you have. If you take classes, don't shy away from opportunities to perform for your peers. You can gain a lot from performing in a supportive environment without feeling as timid. Don't feel bad if you're not the most celebrated singer or performer in the class. I must reiterate for you that it does not matter how "talented" people think or say you are or are not. You can perform and find your own niche and become a star, or at least gain confidence in your abilities.

## Find an Opportunity to Sing

Before you even graduate from school, you should try to be aware of opportunities to learn music as part of your school curriculum. I was able to obtain a lot of live singing experience in high school choir classes.

*Join a choir*

## Choir as a Great Place to Begin

In junior high and high school choir, I learned about harmony, melody, range, and different voice types. I learned about the difference between singing solo and singing with a group, where you must blend in with the other singers, not dominate them. In addition to this, I was able to perform live with my high school choir.

We had a great teacher who arranged for us to perform wherever possible. We performed at malls, store openings, and an Easter sunrise service. The choir had to start singing before dawn and continue as the sun rose on Easter Sunday.

Though I never had any solos, choir gave me a chance to sing confidently within a structured setting. If I sang a wrong note, no one would have noticed. This is a healthy environment for anyone to start singing in; it promotes positivity and friendliness with other people who love singing. This is a fantastic confidence builder. I highly recommend it for anyone at any age who wants to sing. I cannot stress enough how important it is for you to start singing in front of some type of audience.

Choir can be a great place to start, and even spend a lifetime dedicated to, but what if you don't want to stay there?

## When I Realized It Was Time for Me to Leave Choir

There was an opportunity to be a soloist in our high school choir. This was a coveted position which only went to seniors. Though I was only in the ninth grade, I auditioned for it anyhow. The choir director told me that he thought I had the best voice but that because the solo position only ever went to seniors, I, like everyone else in that choir before me, would have to wait until I was a senior.

That meant it would be another three years before I would get my chance. There were no opportunities for me to sing solo, which was what I wanted to do. This ushered in the end of my choir singing.

Prior to this, I had been in a show at my junior high school where I sang two solos and received a standing ovation. It seems surreal now. As an overweight kid from a single parent household without the same resources most of the other kids had, this was one of my first memories of real acceptance. People's parents wanted to meet me, popular kids at school came up and congratulated me. Few people had ever shown me that much positive attention before (except my wonderful and encouraging mom).

I knew that singing was what I really wanted to do. So, flash forward to ninth-grade choir when I was told I would have to wait years for another solo opportunity. I started hating choir!

I believe that if you don't like something, you shouldn't do it. You shouldn't stay in a situation that doesn't benefit you. I understand that this runs counter to what many people, institutions, and teachers tell you.

I have probably changed jobs more than a hundred times. I've done a lot of temp work for big companies between my singing and acting jobs. I'm so glad I never accepted the many full-time jobs offered to me by big companies like Warner Bros. Records or Fuji Film. Don't trade your dreams for the day job if that's not what you want.

## If It's Not Right for You, Don't Do It

Do what you love! If you love something, it's for a reason. When the next school year began, I decided to get into the school plays where I would have a better chance of singing solo. And I did! By changing my focus from choir to theatre, I gained access to more resources, different teachers and directors to learn from, and new knowledge from what I had learned in choir.

## Jump In!

A few years later the choir broke with tradition and let the younger students sing that solo anyway. I could have spent all those years in choir waiting and hoping for my opportunity, only to lose it to a freshman. I'm so glad I looked for other opportunities and did not wait in choir for a turn that might have never come.

You may find it refreshing to examine other possibilities available to you. There are many teachers along life's path; staying with any of them for too long can lead to stagnation.

## Free or Low-Cost Resources

Take a closer look at extra-curricular programs you may not have realized existed. I don't recommend rushing to hire a private teacher if it's not the only option available to you and may not even be the best option for you.

Of course, many public schools, community colleges, and university extension programs offer great courses for people of any age. I got a lot out of these programs; maybe you will too.

## My First Professional Singing Jobs

When I was in high school, people in my mom's apartment building started asking me to sing for their functions, like weddings. This was great for me. It usually consisted of a few songs, mostly ballads. People were always very supportive about my singing. These were my first professional performing experiences. By this time, I had spent years getting all I could from the public school system, which had given me an excellent framework to continue developing my own musical interests. This cannot be overstated. If you want as much singing experience as possible, don't dismiss opportunities which may be available to you at no cost or little cost.

I was practicing singing one day when someone knocked on the door. It was a friend of one of the people who lived in the apartments. He had heard me practicing with some rock music (Pat Benatar). He complimented me and asked me to join his band. Yes, I joined my first band because someone heard me practicing in my mom's apartment!

## Unexpected Difficulties

By this time, I had devoted much of my young life to singing, and although I had already spent many years performing, I had no idea how to perform in a band.

I stood singing with my eyes closed and did not know the first thing about non-choir or non-theatre related movement. After a few rehearsals, I still could not get the hang of performing a song with a band onstage, so they let me go!

## Different Types of Singing

This is when I learned that choir is very different from theatre, and theatre is very different from solo singing, and solo singing is very, VERY different from performing in a band.

Different types of singing require different mindsets and skill sets. Another problem was that I had never been expected to sing so many songs before. I wanted to be accepted by the musicians and give it my all every time, so I tried to sing every song with my full voice.

While I could do it, it was hard and sometimes made me hoarse. I was confused! I did not love theatre or choir and I did not see any other opportunities to sing the way I wanted to.

At this point, there were no more helpful guides to show me how to become a recording artist, which was what I wanted to be. I had to think of another way. I wanted to be a big star like the people I heard on the radio and practiced along with all those years. Radio music was omnipresent, yet there were no schools or helpers to teach me how to have a career in that field.

## More Learning and Difficulties

Flash forward a few years to when I was about 18 years old. During high school, I had taken some theatre dance classes at the local community college to improve my performing skills. I love dancing, but I have a hard time remembering the moves. I am that one kid in the group who moves left when everyone else moves right.

I'm pretty sure a few of my ballet, jazz, and tap dance teachers slapped their faces wondering why I could not remember the moves. I sure did try though, because I always loved dancing and still do, but like lines in a play, I could not seem to remember dance move sequences.

Even though I was in a lot of plays, I had a lot of trouble remembering my lines. No matter how hard I tried, I would almost always experience that moment of terror when someone's line had just finished and I could not remember my next line. This happened more than once. Despite trying very hard, I forgot lines and choreographed dance moves so often that theatre and dance became a nightmare.

## Part of Learning What You Want to Do is Learning What You Don't Want to Do

The next stage of my learning involved taking an excellent set of college courses. These included live performance of pop and jazz music and an especially terrific studio recording program. Unlike today where you can record at home and get a decent sound, back then this was an expensive thing to do. They had a full recording studio where they could record high-quality songs.

Never had I taken a course which was so relevant to what I wanted to do! This training was fantastic because it focused on what someone interested in singing pop music as a career would need to know.

## More Problems

I also took music theory and piano classes while there. However, I could never understand math or written music. I learned a bit about it in choir, but I never became a good sight reader. This is a requirement for a studio singer. I could never get the hang of it, so I left that class.

As with all the instruments I had tried before (except for my early experience with the autoharp), I couldn't understand the piano or keyboard, so I also dropped out of piano class. I felt like I was putting undue pressure on teachers when I asked too many questions. I think they thought I was trying to waste their time. However, I liked them, and I respect what they do.

## Teachers Are Just People

Some are quick to blame teachers when students are unable to absorb the information they are teaching. However, teachers may be trying as hard as they can, and they might get tired of trying to teach you! They are JUST PEOPLE who took a series of courses to get a degree for a job.

Just like anyone else, a teacher might be able to help you and they might be sympathetic to your needs. However, if they are not, or you do not get what you are seeking, **release them from your high expectations**. Look elsewhere.

This was the case with my dance teachers. Some politely endured my lack of ability and others were openly insulting towards me. However, they are not the ultimate test of you or your talent.

I've probably done more professional dancing than almost any of those teachers. Being a teacher is good, but remember this, it is **not** *actually performing!*

I learned not to expect too much from teachers, and while I did drop out of some college courses, I got a lot out of others. The live performance and microphone technique classes and the recording classes I took were indispensable.

## In the Recording Studio

Another college class which would prove beneficial to my future career as a music producer and composer was the music writing and recording program. I met a lot of great people there, one of whom was an amazing songwriter who allowed me to sing and co-write some of his songs.

My music friends and I wrote and recorded a few songs. One of them had what was a pretty good home set up at the time. He allowed me to write my own lyrics to his music, so I finally had some recorded music to show people. This is much easier to obtain now than it was when I was 19. Also, on the college's CD recording program, I was credited as a writer and had other people sing songs I had written. What a fresh experience! After this, I was sure that I wanted to sing live and become a recording artist.

This gave me direction and a path into the world I wanted to be in. A door opened which had not existed for me before. I continued to record songs with my friend and found other recording opportunities with other producers. I made demo "mixtapes" of original material which showcased my voice. This gave me something to show people; without it they never would have hired me.

After this, I performed in more bands, did more gigs, traveled, and worked as a pro. I have been fortunate enough to work with some of the top musicians in the fields of recording and touring and privileged enough to get on stage with some living legends.

## When to Leave the Nest of Academia?
## YOU Must Decide When to Step Up to the Mic

*Corded microphone*

I like academia, but I don't like to stay there for too long. I always want my art to make money, so I never did any free gigs after high school or joined any hobbyist groups. I always got paid for my live performing or recording in some way. Many people have a hard time knowing when to leave the world of the paying customer (student) and step into the world of the paid singer (professional). It feels strange at first, but once you do a few paid jobs, you will get more.

Some people never get past the idea that they must do everything perfectly. No matter how hard you try or how well received your work is, it will never be perfect. In addition to judging yourself, in the huge chasm between good and good enough lies another tough thing to deal with, and that is public acceptance or criticism. We'll discuss that more later. For now, let's get started practicing your songs!

# Vocal Teachers: My Advice

# Chapter 4a
# A Basic Framework for Practicing

People tend to think that if you learn to "sing," you can instantly sing anything. Suddenly you will be able to step right up to a microphone and flawlessly belt out any tune. That's simply not true.

More than anything, you need to spend quality time with the material you plan to sing. One of the biggest tips I can give you or anyone who wants to sing is to follow the steps below.

## The Basic Framework for Practice

1. Whenever you plan to sing publicly, try to get a backing track of your chosen song to practice with or sing along to the original recording. Karaoke style backing tracks are helpful for this. They can be purchased in music stores or online. They are a great tool for practicing and can even be used for public performances. I have used backing tracks for some performances, particularly solo and duo acts.

2. Choose a song you like. It's great if you have a real reason to practice it. I advocate getting involved in as many opportunities to sing as possible. Pick a song and start working on it every day if you can.

3. Begin with the simple vocal exercises outlined in this book. Don't get too hung up on the exercises. They can be tedious and take up too much time. You just need to get yourself

## A Basic Framework for Practicing

warmed up. Then move on to the actual song because the song is everything.

4. After practicing the song all the way through once or twice, audio record yourself. You can, and should, video record too, but for now, let's just focus on the sound. How you look and what you do on stage is important but it is not the song. For now, just focus on listening to yourself in your audio playback until you get the song right.

5. Sing the song through once or twice without recording. Then when you record yourself, listen back and take note of the parts you do not like.

   Try to get on with the practicing within ten minutes; you don't want your voice to cool down. You might be surprised to learn that the parts you're having trouble with are consistently concentrated in the same areas, on the same words, or the same consonants or vowel sounds. Once you have identified the parts that could use improvement, **work on those parts only**. Do not practice the whole song. Only work on the parts you are having trouble with.

   I want to repeat that. Practice those problem areas and find a way to make them sound as good as you can, any way you can, as quickly as you can!

6. After spending some time (20 or 30 minutes at most) working on the parts you did not like, sing the song again all the way through and record yourself one last time. Listen to your improvement. This kind of rehearsing maximizes time and

vocal stamina. It gets the song you plan to perform in a "ready to go" state much more quickly than other methods.

It's important to not just sing, but to listen closely to what you are singing. Once you fix the parts you do not like, you may be surprised at how much more confidence you have and how great the parts you do like sound.

## My Mom's Musical Influence

Incidentally, my mom was somewhat of an early vocal coach for me. She did not give me pie in the sky ideas about how my talent was better than anyone else's but she loved my singing and song writing.

Sometimes when I practiced while she was home she would submit the occasional comment. Every now and then, if she did not like a note I sang, I would hear a painful "noooo," but she was very encouraging and I respected her opinion.

One of the reasons I respected my mom's opinions about my singing was her musical past. In high school, she played clarinet and was compared to Benny Goodman, a master clarinetist and bandleader of the WWII era. Although she did not choose to pursue music professionally, she knew her stuff!

Most often her comments were positive. In a world of criticism, my mom provided the positivity I needed to believe in myself. She was my number one fan.

Even though I valued my mom's input, it could be distracting sometimes, so from an early age I learned to practice alone. My latchkey days were helpful for this as I was often alone in the apartment before she got home. I could practice every day after school, and I did. I practiced singing to both female and male singers. You may be surprised to find that your range is capable of singing material written for both females and males, so practice with both. If it's out of your range, don't strain, but try to go as far up and down with the singer's voice as is comfortable for you.

## Tips for Improving Problem Areas

Now you know my basic framework for practice, but what if you can't figure out how to make those bad parts sound better? Below are a few of the best tips I can give for this.

## Experiment with Alternate Vowel Sounds

Vowels can offer different ways to pronounce the same word. If you are having trouble singing a specific word, try swapping out the vowel sounds. For instance, Mariah Carey (who is beyond incredible in my book) sometimes chooses to use alternate vowel sounds. Sometimes she pronounces the word "me" like "may." This changes the vowel sound she has to sing from an E sound to an A sound. It still sounds great in the recording!

This may sound silly, but it's one of the best ways to clear up any parts of a song you can't seem to fix. Humans are not made of wood or brass like instruments. Our vocal cords cannot always sing every vowel sound of every word, in every key, the same, or even at all.

So, if you're having trouble with a particular part of a song, take a look at these guys:

A, E, I, O, U

Then consider alternate sounds for each. Experiment with different sounds and remember that they may not always sound natural to you, but within the context of the song, they may be an effective way to deliver a line.

If you have worked on a song and there is just a part, a word, a note, or a sequence of notes that don't work for you, but you like the song overall, try some of these alternatives.

## Examine the Parts Right Before and After the Part You Have Trouble With

Sometimes the reason we cannot sing a part in a song is not actually because of that part, but because of the parts *directly before or after it*. So, examine the parts around the part you're having trouble with. Often, it's because we need to take a deeper breath ahead of time to finish the phrase with enough strength. Practicing the entire song without stopping will help you figure out where to take breaths without sounding unnatural.

Recording yourself will also help you find out where the best and most natural places are within a song to take those much-needed breaths, which will help you give your best performances.

## Your Lungs and Diaphragm Are Secret Weapons

Without worrying too much about breathing correctly, try to make sure that when you begin a phrase you've taken a big enough breath to **control those notes and push them through**. Squeeze the breath out of your lungs, pushing with your stomach as you sing out. Try to get the last breath out and complete that note, word, or phrase.

Some of the best singing tips seem simple or silly, but this is one of the biggest keys: Use your lungs and diaphragm! If you are having trouble with a part in a song, pre-think where you will need to take an extra breath and then... use it! Remember it like a magic spell. Push that oxygen out of you and get those notes out. When you think it's all gone, push the breath out more. Call upon your lungs and your diaphragm to make your voice more powerful. This especially helps with softer notes which can sometimes be harder to sing than louder ones. This is also the key to sustaining longer notes.

## Pre-Plan When to Breathe

To master any song, pre-think your breathing line by line. Identify which lines require a deeper breath to sustain you through that part. Sometimes it will seem as though there is no opportunity for a breath in between a few long lines, but you must find a way to get that breath. Planning when to breathe head of time can make all the difference.

# Chapter 4b
# Simple Exercises and Tips on Posture & Breathing

[Refer to bonus audio portion for exercise examples: https://soundcloud.com/jason_randall/01-sing-now-exercise-examples]

Growing up I never had access to a piano. I don't want you to need an instrument to do exercises. I want you to remove as many obstacles to singing as possible. After I taught my students a few basic exercises, I requested that they come to class already warmed up, so we could concentrate on the songs.

As I've mentioned many times in this book, I do not concentrate much on vocal exercises. My approach focuses on performance. Exercises, although important, are secondary.

Below are a few vocal exercises for you to try. As I've said, you can find many more great exercises online and elsewhere, but these are the ones I prefer.

1. Bbbbb: This one is my favorite and the one I use most often before gigs. Listen to your voice for any "breaks" or "cracks" on the way up or down. This exercise is great to get everything nice and smooth from top to bottom. Do it a few times and you will most likely smooth out the difficult areas. I have to touch the tip of my nose to do this exercise, otherwise it tickles.

2. Ahhhh: This is another great one. When you do this one, try to open your mouth so that your jaw is as wide as it can be. Concentrate on opening your jaw vertically, don't worry as much about opening it horizontally. Imagine how it feels before you yawn. Start at your highest note and Ahhhh your way down to your lowest notes. This is to loosen your jaw and you will probably feel it in your ears too.

3. Nnnnn: This is the same idea but with the consonant N. Take it from the bottom to the top and back to the bottom. You will feel a "buzz" in the mask of the face for this one.

4. Vowels: Finally, this is the same basic idea as the above exercises, but now do each vowel sound separately and, as before, start at the bottom of your comfortable range and go up to the top and back down again. Remember how I said if you can't sing a particular note on a particular vowel to experiment with other vowels? This can better acquaint you with which vowels are easier or harder for you.

There are many great coaches and YouTube videos which can show you more vocal exercises. However, doing the above exercises can get you quickly warmed up for the real practice, which should be the actual song you are working on.

## Posture

Posture is very important for singing... and it's not.

I know people will give me trouble for this as it is true that your breath and body can deliver notes more clearly with a singer's posture. However, watch any live performer; there is no way they can perform a song believably while standing in an optimum singer's posture for very long.

I'm mentioning body alignment here because it's one of those things that's good to "get it and forget it." Don't worry as much about your posture as your song and giving a great and natural performance.

Here it is:

1. Stand up straight with your feet about eight inches apart, pointed straight.

2. Situate your pelvis in the middle of where your feet are. Don't push it too far forward or back. Tighten your stomach and upper body to feel the center of your strength. Acquaint yourself with the strength in your lungs and diaphragm.

3. Bring your shoulders back a little and pull your chin in slightly.

I personally do not like having to think about posture when I am performing so I try to hold my body in this position every now and then throughout the day for a few seconds or so. It's easy to do it in line at the grocery store, for instance. If you pay more attention to your posture periodically throughout the day, it will become automatic and you won't have to think about it when you sing.

## Singing Is Breathing

# Simple Exercises and Tips on Posture & Breathing

When it comes to singing, there is nothing more important or beneficial than taking control of your full ability to breathe. I've studied with vocal coaches who taught me about "lower diaphragmatic breathing" and I wholeheartedly endorse it.

At first I found it hard to tell whether I was doing it right or not. Usually, when a vocal coach teaches you about this kind of breathing, they put their hand on your stomach while you breathe and tell you when you're doing it right.

Knowing whether you're using your lower diaphragmatic breathing when you are singing can be hard. If you have ever played a trumpet or saxophone, you understand that you must push the air through with strength to pull the notes from the instrument.

It is the same concept for singers, but most singers don't think of having to push air through their bodies like a trumpet player would. I use my trumpet for parts in my songs, and while I am no great trumpet soloist, I can get a strong sound out of it. Thinking of yourself as playing a trumpet can be a good way to mentally prepare yourself for singing.

By the way, breath control is important for singing both loud and soft notes. If you are a rapper, accessing enough oxygen to sustain you through all those words can often be harder than singing.

The breathing tips listed below illustrate as best I can in writing how it feels to sing using the muscles of your lower diaphragm.

1. To feel the diaphragm, try this. Lightly cough a few times. It is almost impossible not to feel your lower diaphragm and stomach muscles at least a little. Now you know what that feeling is.

2. Now that you know the area where you want to focus your breath strength, exhale all the oxygen in your lungs. When you think all the air is gone, find more by pushing it out with your lower stomach muscles. Pay no attention to your lungs at all. Act as though only your stomach muscles hold air and push it all out.

3. Inhale deeply over a ten count. Again, imagine that you are filling your stomach with air, starting from roughly where your belly button is. Don't fill the upper lungs with oxygen until your tummy feels completely full of oxygen. Hold your shoulders back to allow your lungs to open, but do not raise them if possible. This forces you to pay closer attention to the section below the lung area.

4. Now push the air out in separate small but forceful gusts, making a "huh" sound each time, as though you are coughing or having a belly laugh. Expel all the oxygen this way.

5. Now you have a better idea of the feeling you are going for when you use your lower diaphragm for breathing, rather than just the power of your lungs. Think of your lungs as a holding tank for oxygen but think of your lower stomach muscles as the power.

I want to stress again that any exercises or tips are only secondary and if you have to think about them too much, you can't devote yourself completely to your performance.

## The Tip You Won't Believe

Are you ready for the weirdest tip ever?

Remind yourself of this...

## Most of the time when you are performing live, the audience is not really listening!

This may sound like a load of malarkey, but any musician or singer who has performed live for any length of time will chuckle at this statement, knowing it to be the truth.

Most of the time when you are performing professionally you will be in an environment where people are not necessarily there to see *you* or any of the other musicians in the band. Most of the time, they are attending a function of some sort, having fun in a nightclub, attending a private party, etc. You may find that it does not matter that you just sang your best rendition of Whitney Houston's biggest hit, and gave it your all, to no applause.

Further still is the shock you may experience when Mark on the drums makes a huge mistake, or Bob on guitar plays the wrong notes in his solo, or Dave on keys just gave a Hollywood Bowl worthy solo, but the audience's response is the same for each!

This is because, aside from a few music lovers, very few people are **actually listening**. You may be shocked to find that people are equally oblivious to the playing ability of musicians and the vocal ability of singers.

As long as the players and singers look and act professional and stay relatively close to the basic harmonic and melodic parts of the song they are performing, there is nothing for the audience to be distracted by and no one notices.

For instance, people who came to the nightclubs on the cruise ships I worked on to see the showband were not there to see us. They were there to get sloshed and have a good time. Respect that and realize that you're there to help them have fun. Try to be positive and upbeat. Don't expect them to pay attention to your performance as they would at a concert.

Even Celine Dion mentioned in an interview that the people who attended her Las Vegas residency performances were not her normal fan base. I know the crowd she's talking about. Those people were in Las Vegas looking for something to do. They probably had just come from a huge buffet and were sleepy. They wanted to see a show that night and it may have been between Celine, Shania, Wayne Newton, etc. This was not a pilgrimage to see Celine. They were not watching with the same love that people who go to see Celine's arena concerts are.

It's sad for some artists to find out, but it can also be empowering to know that if you make mistakes, it's likely no one will notice. Now that you know, let's keep that top secret between you and me! No one likes to think that they can't tell what good music or musicians are.

## Case Study: A Virtuoso in a Subway

To further illustrate this point, The Washington Post conducted a Pulitzer Prize-winning social experiment involving virtuoso violinist Joshua Bell. This world-famous, Grammy-winning, Carnegie Hall violinist agreed to perform in a busy subway with his case open to accept tips, just days after selling out a concert in Boston with $100 seats.

Bell brought his 3.5 million dollar, handcrafted, 1713 Stradivarius violin and played his heart out performing some of the world's greatest compositions in classical music for 45 minutes.

By the end of the set, thousands of people had passed him by. He made $32.17 and gained the attention of practically no one, other than a few small children who had to be pulled along by their parents.

Bell was not playing at Carnegie Hall this time, where everyone felt confident saying he was great. His talents were devalued because of the "frame" of the subway, instead of the "frame" of Carnegie Hall. Most people were afraid to praise, or even pause for, this violinist because he must not be that good if he's in a subway, right? Wrong!

## Take That Advice to the Bank and Cash It

Remember, most people don't know as much about music as they like to think and can't really tell whether it's good or bad. Besides, who can judge art anyway?

I'm going out on a limb with some of my advice here, but I've worked enough as a professional singer in enough different venues to know what I'm talking about. I hope this can give you more confidence to perform. You don't have to be perfect all the time.

# Chapter 5
# Respecting All Music

I love pop music and always have. I could never understand why people always put it down the first chance they got. Teachers, musicians, and regular people often have something bad to say about pop music.

Yet, it is ubiquitous and remains... popular. Whether you notice it or not, you hear pop music on in-store radio, in hotel lobbies, restaurants, etc. You may not know who Pharrell is, but I bet you know his song "Happy."

People profess to know everything about music. What's good, what's bad, why their music is so much better than the "crap" that's out there today, blah blah blah. The first thing many musicians and singers do when discussing music is criticize pop music and pop stars. Yet this music exists for a reason; **the world loves it!**

Humans are motivated by many of the elements in pop music. People mistakenly believe that the finely crafted, catchy music on the radio is written by the artist who performs it. In reality, most of the best selling songs you've heard for decades were written by the same veteran writers.

> *"I'm personally looking for artists that are along the lines of today's pop stars. Whether it be a Rihanna or a Justin Bieber or a Kanye West or a Beyonce or a Lady Gaga, I'm looking for talent that's like that, that's what I love."*

- L.A. Reid, celebrity music executive

## Sing What You Like

A lot of teachers would have you singing only classical music pieces and disregarding other styles, including pop. However, I've found that most people don't want to sing the kind of songs a lot of vocal coaches want them to sing. I advocate singing what you truly love to keep your enthusiasm for music as rich as possible.

## Daycare DJ

When I was a young child, I was in a daycare program where we had an afternoon nap time with music in the background. Sometimes we brought in our own music. It was mostly sleepy nursery rhyme stuff - the kind of music that babies love but quickly grow out of.

Don't get me wrong, I love the nursery rhyme stuff. In fact, I've composed many pieces of children's music, some of which have been in toy ads and children's audio products. However, I have found that most kids crave something else.

At about age five, I brought in music from my own collection. The lyrics were about the Flintstones, but the music style was upbeat and pop rock. All the kids loved it! I think they were somewhat relieved to not have to listen to baby music. I was the hero for a while; the kids only wanted to listen to my Flintstones album during nap time for weeks. I've never forgotten that experience.

## Some Things Never Change

Flash forward to my vocal coaching days. Like myself, my students were hungry for today's pop music.

> *"All Children are artists. The problem is how to remain an artist once he grows up."*
>
> - Pablo Picasso, world-famous artist

This is what makes them enthusiastic about singing. They love the pop songs and the pop stars.

I have seen children forced into singing something they don't like for the sake of "getting better." Often this dampens their love for music and singing. Pop, rock, soul, hip-hop, rap - all these genres are popular because people love them.

Children (and most people) would rather listen to pop music than theatre, opera, classical, instrumental, or jazz. Yes, even the most acclaimed music does not receive the same love (or dollars) as good old pop music that no one ever admits to loving, except the children.

Try not to criticize anyone else's music, even if others do. People do this to make themselves seem smarter or more cultured, but in reality it just makes them ignorant.

## A Word about Rap

I LOVE rap music. Over the years I've come to learn a few things about rapping. Even if you don't rap on most of your songs, you may find that it is good to know how to rap sometimes. Many modern songs contain rap parts which you may have to perform as part of your job, so here are a few tips to deliver rap lyrics.

## Rapping Is Not Talking

Rapping requires a more percussive and deliberate stress on individual words. If you don't do this, your words can sound slurred and connected. You need the words to sound **separate.** Try to give each word its own gust of breath.

Enunciate each word firmly without yelling. Rapping too loudly can cause feedback in the microphone, so you have to balance it.

Avoid "plosives," or extra mouth sounds from loudness which can sound like distortion. Watch for the consonant "P" and substitute it with a "B" if you must.

If some of your words get buried, it can be helpful to increase your voice's high end. This manifests itself in the "mask" of the face and can require a more nasal delivery to be heard well, so experiment with tones when you practice.

## Microphone Technique

Do not hold the microphone on the top part or anywhere near the input area at the top of the microphone. This causes feedback and can ruin the whole performance. Do not point the microphone downward as this can also cause feedback which takes a few minutes to remedy, and while you are on stage it can ruin the performance.

*Ludacris*

In this photo, rapper Ludacris shows you how NOT to hold a microphone in most live music settings. When rappers do concerts, they have sound people who adjust their microphone levels ahead of time. If you are rapping as part of a song you are performing, you will not hold the microphone this way.

## Be Aware of Your Highs and Lows

If you are rapping at a higher intensity in one part of a song, move your mouth further away from the mic. If you are rapping at a lower intensity, bring your mouth closer to the mic.

Attitude goes well with rapping, so if you can pull out your inner Nicki Minaj, your delivery will be better-received. Whatever you do, don't be afraid of rap. When you have a chance to rap, walk up to that mic and give it all the attitude and strength you have.

*Nicki Minaj*

"You're not going to tell me who I am, I'm going to tell you who I am."

- Nicki Minaj, rap superstar

# Chapter 6
# Singing in a Recording Studio

One day you might have a chance to sing in a recording studio. Nowadays, you may have your own home studio where you can write and record music. Back in the day, that was not available to most people.

I was lucky enough to work in a few recording studios. I worked with one producer for over a year whose work I loved. He had already had credits writing a song for a well-known group. He had written some great songs and needed a singer. He liked my voice and we produced an EP extended play album. It took months to get the vocals right for each song. For the first time, I had a clear idea of how perfect the voice needs to be when you record multiple tracks in the studio.

This producer was a nice person but brutally honest about the sound he wanted for his music. I spent a lot of time having to redo things I thought I had nailed earlier on. I had been singing and recording for years by this time, and I thought he was being too picky, but when I listened back carefully, I realized I was not hitting the notes as well as I thought.

I was flat or sharp in between some notes. For me (and this may be the case for you as it's a common pitfall in singing), it was the transitional notes between the bigger words that I had trouble with. I had been covering this up with style, concentrating on singing loud and strong, or soft and breathy. If I did not take extra care sometimes I was either a little flat or a little sharp on the quicker notes. I don't want you to worry too much about this right now; being too worried about anything can suck the joy out of it.

My point is that it is good to take into consideration that singing well might allow you to get away with some bad notes, but in a studio environment, you do not have the benefit of people being distracted from your voice by watching you on stage. Unlike a live performance where people mostly "listen with their eyes," in the recording studio, people can't see you. They must rely on their ears.

For studio singing, it's useful to remember these tips.

## Studio Singing Is Not Live Singing

Sometimes it is necessary to sing the same song differently in the studio than you would for a live performance.

Studio microphones are typically more sensitive to changes in the dynamics of your voice.

Studio microphones can more easily read your volume as loud, "top out," known as "clipping," and become distorted in the mix. Practice your song ahead of time for recording, keeping this in mind.

## The Pop Screen

There is usually a light mesh barrier separating the performer's mouth from the microphone. This can help with some issues like popping "P" sounds, lingering "S" sounds, and sharp "T" sounds.

*Little boy with pop screen*

The little boy in the illustration above is using a pop screen. However, he's probably going to top out and get distortion (clipping) in his recording because he looks like he's singing way too loud.

## Beware the Noisy Clothing Monster

Some clothing is very noisy. A lot of jackets (especially leather) can squeak and rustle around as you move along to the music. This means you will have to remove whatever is causing any excess noise. This includes things like loud earrings, bangle bracelets, etc. Even your hair can sometimes be heard moving against a collar. Try to keep this in mind and deal with it beforehand to avoid embarrassment. Singers who hold up the recording session for any reason usually don't get called back.

## Beware the Noisy Tummy Monster

Make sure you've eaten something. This may sound funny, but if you go to a recording session and have not eaten for a while, your tummy may tell on you! It might growl, gurgle, or make other unflattering noises which can be picked up clearly by the microphones.

This has happened to me. I was recording a song for Japanese retail outlets. The recording studio was in Hollywood and I was almost late because of traffic. I had forgotten to eat anything and my stomach would not stop talking. I was lucky the producer was understanding and worked around the weird sounds my stomach made. Keep some nuts or trail mix in your bag so this silly but common thing does not happen to you.

## Double Your Vocals

Doubling makes recordings sound more powerful and solid. When I first started working and recording in studios and with individuals, I had mainly worked on stage, in live singing situations. I was surprised to find that one of the most common practices in recording is to "double" most or all of your vocal parts.

This means that for everything you sing, you will probably lay down another vocal track which will be mixed with your first track. You will have to match your previous recording as closely as possible. Many differences can be heard clearly when your doubling is "off."

How do you remedy this? Well, it's back to our old friend Rehearsal Time! If you have a good idea of how you will be singing the song and you have practiced it ahead of time, it will be easier to match the lengths of your lines, your volume, your style, etc. Having to keep repeating something again and again because you can't remember how you did it on the earlier take is not fun.

## Vocal Practice Review

In chapter four of this book, I went over the steps I use to practice singing. As I've said before, my method is to:

1. Do your exercises for about ten minutes. Use the basic tips provided in this book or exercises from anywhere you like.

2. Sing your song once or twice through.

3. Sing your song again, this time recording it.

4. Play it back and make a note of the problem areas, then work on those parts only. For instance, if you can't sing that note in that key, try to use a harmony note, or try experimenting with alternate vowel sounds, using more breath, and pre-thinking where to breathe.

5. Do not give up! Find a way to sing or at least satisfactorily deliver the parts you have trouble with. This prepares you for what you will do on the hardest parts of the song. Once you have conquered these, the song will feel more comfortable.

6. Practice the song again, the entire way through, recording yourself again.

7. Play it back to see if your performance has improved. If not, you can continue working on the song or resume the same practice the next day. However, avoid burning out. A half hour to an hour a day is good for a beginner, especially if you are teaching yourself. Sometimes a teacher can help you and prevent you from hurting your vocal cords. If you want to continue practicing, by all means, do. However, stop if you become hoarse or uncomfortable.

## Why Is this Type of Practice so Important?

Doing this exercise will improve your performance of the song and give you confidence. You will be ready to sing it with minimal rehearsal in the future. This means you can add it to your *repertoire*.

## Building Your Repertoire

This is how you start building your repertoire, which is a concrete step toward being ready to sing when opportunities arise. After adding a few songs to your repertoire, you will be much more confident to perform.

I've missed opportunities because I was not prepared, and I know you have too - we all have. Being prepared with rehearsed material is one of the biggest steps toward working professionally in music.

This is still the way I work in new songs and it never ends. It is unusual for anyone, even a trained opera star, to get up on a stage and sing a random song without ever having rehearsed it before. Each song you plan to perform requires its own rehearsal for your best performances to shine through.

## Percussion Instruments

I first picked up the tambourine, then shakers, and eventually a lot more percussion instruments. I advocate that you take a chance with them as well. Play along with yourself while you are singing. It may seem hard at first, but if you can work in percussion as part of your act (and do it well), you can develop a closer relationship with rhythm.

## She Wowed the Crowd

One of my students, an adorable eight-year-old, was set to perform for her upcoming recital. I chose the song "Hit the Road Jack" by Ray Charles for her to sing. She sang marvellously and I wondered if she could work in playing the tambourine as well. I showed her a few simple rhythmic patterns and she took to them right away.

The audience loved her performance, but they gasped with astonishment when she simultaneously sang and played the tambourine. I never suggested to her that it was hard; I presented it to her like, "here, try this and see if it's fun." Maybe you will find it fun and be a natural like her.

# Chapter 7
# Stage Etiquette: Being Professional to All the Players (Even If You Don't Get Along)

Everyone on stage with you has a right to his or her own expression of the music you are performing. It's also important to remember that your audience experiences all of you together as one unit.

Sometimes a band member might call attention to another band member's mistake by looking at them onstage and making faces, gestures, or otherwise calling attention to their blunder.

In this situation, it's likely that the audience has no idea that anyone made a mistake and the band member giving the looks is being unprofessional and rude by trying to expose someone else's weak moment.

The most professional way to deal with a situation like this is to keep smiling and avoid doing anything to make the person look or feel bad. In fact, if you keep smiling and performing as though nothing happened, you're helping to save everyone.

Similarly, if you don't get along with another player on stage and you avoid looking at them, or you frown at them, etc., the audience **will** see that.

For the sake of the whole band, know that if any of the players look unprofessional, the entire group loses face. For pros, it's not about attitude, it's about **getting paid.** Try never to compromise that.

*Me with one of my earliest groups*

Can't you tell that Bob is frowning and sulking while the rest of us are working hard?!

# Chapter 8
# Why It Hurts You to Criticize Others

To perform at all, whether it's signing, acting, dancing, speaking, or anything else, takes courage. Many people cannot understand why you want to perform.

Once you start to do unusual things like dare to sing solo on a stage, some people will not be happy about your efforts toward your dreams. It can sometimes feel as though you're offending them by being yourself and working toward your goals.

Understand that people's criticism is not always a genuine critique of your talent. Most people ready to criticize you don't have any knowledge in the area you are working in. In my experience, people who are the most accomplished are the slowest to criticize and the first to respect others' work and efforts.

Try not to get caught up in jealousy or judgment of another person's ability. This is a waste of time and will replace your love for music with anger. If you are jealous of another person's success or apparent talent, or you feel that someone less talented than you is getting the attention you deserve, just concentrate on yourself and your own efforts.

The irony is that you are doing it to yourself. You're stealing your own time, wasting your own mental space, and giving your energy away to the person you are judging.

## The Best Singer?

One of my students was a high schooler who had a fantastic voice and seemed to know that. She had a good reputation at her school and a strong opinion of what talent was and was not. She was quite advanced, but she was angry that there was another singer at her school who she felt was getting attention that she did not deserve. She felt this other budding singer was not very talented and was annoyed that she had been given chances to sing. She felt so threatened by her that she spent our valuable class time complaining about her. This other girl's very presence in the arena of singing that my student felt belonged to her was eclipsing her own love for music.

Finally, I told my student that she had to stop worrying about this other girl, that she had a right to sing as much as she did, and that to be so jealous of another person's talent took away from her own time to practice and improve hers.

When you criticize others' efforts, you steal time away from yourself to practice, find new music, enjoy life, see beauty, and experience love. You also put your own mind into a **critical state.** Since you are so critical of others, you find it easier to suspect that others are criticizing you. More of your mind space becomes devoted to anger, hatred, one-upmanship, backbiting, and manipulation. Your negative thoughts become the antithesis of creativity - **criticism.**

My mom used to say, "when they're bothering you, they're giving someone else a break." So, give yourself a break. Have a positive attitude about other people's efforts to improve or learn something new. Even if you don't like what they're doing, does it matter?

The same goes for anything else in any area of your life. Even if you don't like what other people are doing, don't become a curmudgeon. Curmudgeons dedicate their mind and free brain space to sad, negative things.

If someone criticizes you, just let it roll off your back and think about the great possibilities that singing can bring you. It has given me many wonderful things and continues to do so.

If you hope to rise to new heights, do not waste your time criticizing others, or even defending yourself to those who criticize you. If music feels right to you, be courageous and walk on by the "haters." They have chosen their own path, and it's wasting valuable time on hate. What's yours?

## Dealing with Criticism

Don't listen to anyone's criticism unless you truly value it and feel it may help you. Even then, if the criticism of someone you respect makes you feel bad, chuck it as well! Yes, that's right. I'm telling you to NOT take anyone's criticism too seriously, even that of someone you respect. No one knows what the future brings, not even the masters of today.

Tomorrow may reveal a world in which your talents and abilities can flourish. The methods which worked yesterday for your trainers, teachers, or those otherwise deemed "experts," may not be useful in our future world at all.

Try not to assume the worst or react negatively to commentary. Please don't assume that anyone is thinking critical thoughts about you, especially teachers.

I recall another student at one of the classes I took in my youth. The student had finished her song and then received commentary from the teacher. This singer then ran crying from the room. I and some other students did not understand why she did this, as the teacher's commentary was mostly positive. Well, it turned out that she had misheard the teacher, turning a compliment into a condemnation of her efforts. We and the (very nice) teacher tried to set her straight, but she didn't believe us, and if I recall correctly, she left the class soon after.

I want you to examine this situation and think about whether you might be taking ownership of criticism you *think* others have given you. You may be robbing yourself.

## It May Be Best to Keep It to Yourself

Contrary to popular belief, not sharing everything about your singing or the things you are working on can be better than telling everyone you know, or sometimes *anyone* you know.

Telling anyone else about your goals before you have achieved at least some of them leads to people asking, "how's it going?" If you don't have anything to share with them, saying, "nothing is going on" or "I'm having trouble with..." can affect you subconsciously.

However, if you are practicing and trying, you are *improving*, although that may not be apparent yet. Effort is the only way to succeed. You might be on the verge of your biggest breakthrough yet but until that happens it's still a work in progress.

## Remember Van Gogh

Imagine a famous artist like Van Gogh's friends and family insisting that he show every step of his work from the very first outlines. Van Gogh's cousin looks at his sketches and says they don't look like they're any good. Sounds stupid, right? This is what exposing your incubating efforts before they mature is like.

## Your Talent Is a Child

I want you to take yourself and your efforts to sing seriously. Think about a child's efforts to learn to write. They are so proud of their success writing the ABC's. Would you allow an adult to criticize their ABC's because they don't look perfect? Of course not! You would be angry that someone would try to belittle their efforts to grow.

You must protect your talents and efforts as though they were children deserving of time to grow and experiment without the burden of worrying about what others are thinking or living up to anyone else's expectations.

*"Brainwave tests prove that when we use positive words, our 'feel good' hormones flow. Positive self-talk releases endorphins and serotonin in our brain, which then flow throughout our body, making us feel good. These neurotransmitters stop flowing when we use negative words."*

- Ruth Fishel, inspirational author

*Your talent is a child*

You are not obligated to share your fledgling dreams and efforts with anyone. Within a big family, even one negative influence can shut down a person's creativity.

I endured the criticism of others from a young age. I was a heavy-set child and sometimes it was hard to find stylish clothes at a good price, so we often shopped at the thrift store. Green print polyester pants on a heavy-set child will get a snarky remark or even violent threats from their peers, especially if they're a quiet, artistic kid like I was. I was made fun of and treated badly just for being me.

When others heard me sing, most of the time I was criticized or dismissed, but I was eventually accepted by some of the kids who had previously been mean to me. In junior high school, there was a group of girls bothering me in the locker room while I was getting dressed for PE class. One of them had heard me sing before. She stopped them and said, "hey, she sings pretty good. Sing and we won't kick your ass." So, I belted out a popular radio song of the day. Their threatening commentary turned into appreciation for my voice!

After that, they were usually nice to me and this experience made me feel accepted by girls who I had previously been intimidated by. You never know where uplifting experiences will find you. This seemingly dark experience ended up meaning a lot to me and gave me visible evidence that singing had a lot to offer me as it turned some of my toughest critics into supporters.

People say kids are cruel, but adults can also show their critical side with little provocation or consideration for those they're criticizing. I learned that some people would rather spit out a comment like "give it up" than give positive feedback.

This made me aware that even those closest to us, like our friends and relatives, can be this way. Sometimes it's more comfortable for people to know the "You" they already know. When you dare to get up on stage and give it a go, sometimes you awaken the feeling in others that they have given up on their own dreams, or that they are becoming less important to you as you grow.

It's sad, because while you may be supportive of your friends and family who are, say, becoming a teacher, or getting a good job, you may not get the support you feel you should for your dreams.

People are afraid to endorse something unusual. Don't be surprised if you don't get as much support as you give to others. Just go about your work, keep on improving, and don't take it personally.

Don't allow negative attitudes to take up your valuable mind space. Don't forget what my mom told me. "You can do anything you want to do."

# Chapter 9
# Dealing with Stage Fright

*Stage fright*

Stage fright is, well, frightening. Here's a tip that may help you overcome it.

## Sing to the Back Wall

Look at the back of the room, above the audience's heads. Believe it or not, usually people can't tell. It seems like you are looking at them. If it feels more natural for you to look at them, all the better, but if you need help with this from time to time, sing to the back of the room.

## Be Ready with Something to Say

There will be times when you are introduced, come up to the stage ready to perform your song, but then there is dead air because of some unforeseen problem. Guess what? You're already on stage and the audience is looking at you!

While it is possible to look away, run off stage, or talk to the drummer, it's much more engaging to the audience if you talk to them. Talking too much can be annoying to the audience and the band, but talking just enough can win them over before you even start singing.

## Make a Unifying Statement

Acknowledging the event everyone is there for helps. This shows your appreciation for them and the event they chose to spend their time at. Additionally, it's great to mention the town or organization you are performing for. You can thank them over the microphone, showing your appreciation to them and the audience.

## You Forgot the Words, Now What?

What if you make mistakes or feel embarrassed about your performance? It happens to everyone who gets on a stage at some point. You suspect that everyone saw or heard your mistake.

Ignore it and continue as best you can. Do not call attention to it, do not tell the audience about it, and do not apologize. Most importantly, do not stop in the middle of your song or walk off the stage. It does not get worse than that so keep on going with the song until it's over.

Unless something truly dangerous is happening on stage, smile and be gracious even if you felt your performance could have been better. Try not to look visibly upset at what happened. Don't frown or stop or get angry on stage if you feel your performance is not going well. Believe me, I've had some crazy stuff happen to me on stage!

## Memories Light the Corners of My Mind

One of my favorites was when I was performing in Las Vegas. I was singing "Express Yourself" by Madonna. I took a deep breath, and right as I did, a small moth flew in front of my mouth! Before I knew it, he got sucked in. I swallowed, took another breath, and sang the next verse.

## Snot Funny

Here's a good one for you. At one of my gigs I had a cold. I went to sing a note and realized that I had gotten a big piece of snot onto my outfit right on the chest area. It was very visible and as you can imagine, not cute at all. I finished my songs with a smile and removed the snot at the break. I don't know if anyone else saw it; I never asked. Would you?

## Forgetting Words

If you forget the words, simply re-sing the words you do know. If you forget them entirely, you can hum along or ad lib until you remember where you are.

As soon as you realize you're lost in a song, listen for the chorus. Try to identify where the chorus returns in the song and be ready to jump back into the words there. This is one of the best ways to get back on track if you get lost.

You can also choose to "scat" if it's appropriate for the song, in music such as jazz or blues. You can even substitute the lyrics with your own if you need to.

Have you ever seen a performance in which someone sang different lyrics from the ones you know? Did you think they were singing the song wrong? Nope, you thought they were singing additional or alternate lyrics to the song that you did not know.

## More about Talking to the Audience

Even though limited talking is good, if you're lost it may be a good time to talk to the audience. Once again, consider the event and crowd who is in attendance and try to say something meaningful to them.

"Hey Atlanta Baptist Church, do you feel good today?" Compliment them or suggest applause for one of the organizers. For example, "everybody give it up for Sally and Dave, the bride and groom!"

## Briefly Introduce the Band Members

If you're lost, it may be a good time to introduce your band. Gesture over to the keyboard player and say something like, "ladies and Gentlemen, Javier Morales on keys!" Wait a few seconds to a minute, then continue to the rest of the players in the same way. "Mark Wilson on Saxophone." Wait a few seconds to a minute. "Miss Petra Smith on guitar." Wait as before and go through the players, finishing with the drummer. "And finally, rockin' Pete on drums keepin' the beat goin' all night long!" This should get you back to the chorus of the song where you can continue singing. Whew!

## Don't Sweat It, Forget It

Everybody who gets on stage has unexpected challenges. You would be arrogant to assume that every performance you ever give could be perfect in every way. Perfection is not a destination, it's a process.

Remember this: It's the things in life that you DON'T do that you regret, so realize that perfection is a pipe dream and all we can do is love the art enough to never stop trying.

# Chapter 10
# Microphone Types and Technique

There are a variety of microphone techniques for different kinds of microphones. How you hold the microphone may have to do with what kind of microphone it is. For performing live, you will usually use a corded or cordless handheld microphone. Through most of your performance, it's probably good to hold the microphone about two inches from your mouth.

## Avoiding Feedback

Hold the mic about halfway down. Never put your hand over the main part of the microphone as this will usually cause feedback. Never put anything over the top part of the mic; that can cause serious problems. Never point the microphone toward the monitor or other speakers. Doing this will usually cause feedback.

## Corded Microphones

If you have a corded mic (these are still widely used), hold it with your dominant hand and hold the cord with your other hand, in front of you and off to the side. This is so that you do not trip over it as you move around on the stage.

## Cordless Microphones

Cordless microphones (standard today) come with freedom and responsibilities. The funny thing is that corded microphones give you something to do with your other hand, while cordless microphones set that hand free. Free to do what? That's for you to know and for us to find out!

A cordless microphone gives you the freedom to walk around the room if you like. You can go out into the audience and sing to them more closely, invite them to sing along with you, or dance around the stage. For some, a cordless microphone is more of a curse than a blessing. The choice is yours! Here are some things you can do with your free hand:

Hold the microphone with both hands for most of the performance, pulling away one of your hands every now and then to make an expressive gesture at some of the more emotional moments in your song.

Change your microphone hand to sing to the audience on that side of the stage. For instance, look at the left side of the audience while you are singing with your left hand, then move your face and body to the right side of the audience, simultaneously changing to your right hand, giving you maximum audience coverage.

Do the "quiet clap." At some point in the performance, there may be a bridge part or some part which is instrumental. Without touching the microphone, "clap" along to the music. This takes practice because you don't want to hit or slap the microphone, you just want to appear to be grooving along to the music. You can close your eyes and move to the music from time to time, but don't close your eyes too much; it can become a crutch.

## Headset Microphones

If you are in a band or a performance situation that requires you to use a headset microphone, lucky and unlucky you! You will have much more room to move around, but if you're only singing and not dancing much, this kind of microphone can be awkward. It depends on your venue, but usually handheld cordless or corded mics are most effective unless you're going to be performing a lot of dance moves.

*Mic technique*

The vocalist in the picture above demonstrates how to hold the microphone. She is holding it a good distance from her mouth and is holding it in her left hand while singing to the left side of the audience and using her right hand to emote.

## Microphone Technique

Regardless of the kind of microphone you use, you will need to be mindful of technique. Even though I just told you to keep the mic about two inches from your mouth most of the time, I do not mean ALL of the time. There may be differences in the loudness and softness or "dynamic" of your singing.

It takes a little practice to be ready for this when you are performing. After all, singing is emotional but some of the other aspects of performing are technical.

Know ahead of time where the louder notes are in the song. For these parts, you will need to pull the mic further away from your mouth to prevent feedback and preserve the volume of your performance. Also, be aware of where your vocal parts are softer and remember that you may need to bring the microphone a little closer to your mouth for those parts. After a while, these things become second nature.

## Watch Out!

Be on the lookout for obstructions. When performing on stages, there will often be cords taped down underneath where you are standing, monitor speakers in the way, and many more things in your performance space which can be easy to trip and fall on. That's not even funny!

## Microphone Types and Technique

*A stage from above. Look at all those monitors!*

It can be a challenge not to fall on something. Take a few moments before your song to assess the stage or performance space you will be in.

Also, be aware of strange microphone clips. Some can be slid out, some clip on, and some can break easily, sending shattered plastic and coiled springs flying into your face or the audience if it's removed roughly. Look at it before your performance if possible and be gentle with the mic.

## Other Considerations

Listen closely to recordings of pop music you hear on the radio. Notice how you can sometimes hear a soft voice, almost whisper soft, and a loud rap in the same song? In real life, or on a stage, these two volumes would not be perceived by the listener's ears as the same. The producer of the song you hear on the radio has created an environment in which you can listen to a soft voice singing at the same level as a loud rap.

However, when you perform that same song on stage, you will find that such huge volume and percussive differences require some creative microphone technique.

For instance, you need to rap with intensity so that it does not sound like you are just talking, and you need to do this loud enough and percussive enough to be heard well, while avoiding feedback. This is challenging!

It is not natural for someone to be able to sing appropriately for a theater stage, then with a band in a club setting, and then for a studio recording environment, as these are all very different disciplines. However, as difficult as it is to excel in each of these situations, your favorite recording and touring artists must do exactly that to fulfill their contractual obligations.

# Chapter 11
# Basic Movement on Stage

I'm so proud of you for making it this far! Now that the date of your performance, recital, etc. has been chosen, and your song or songs are well rehearsed, your mind and voice are ready! But what should you do with your body when you're on stage?

Even though I had already been in stage shows, performed songs for functions, and had lots of onstage experience singing, when it came to performing material on stage as the **lead singer and the main focus**, I realized I had no idea how to move. Hopefully the following steps can help you avoid that experience.

**I'm on Stage, Now What?**

Try drawing a simple dot-to-dot plan for onstage movement if you don't know what to do.

When you first walk onto the stage, smile and take the mic from the stand. If it seems natural to do so, you can thank the audience. When your song starts playing, sway back and forth to the intro if you feel movement is needed. This should be enough to get you through the instrumental intro and give your body something natural looking to do until you need to start singing.

You can stand in that same spot for part of your song if it feels right. While doing so, slowly look left toward your audience, singing some of the song to that general area. When this feels static, turn your head alone, or your whole body if it feels right, to sing the next part to the audience on the right side.

Usually about a third of the way into your song it will feel natural to walk over to the other side of the stage at a medium pace and sing to the audience there.

Then, about halfway through the song, walk back toward the middle of the stage and deliver some of the song there. Try to make this the "bridge" section which usually occurs about halfway through the song. This might make it easier to coordinate roughly when to move back to the center of the stage.

After the bridge, when you move into another verse or chorus, move toward the other side of the stage and address the right side of the audience.

Lastly, when your song is almost done, move back toward the center and finish off the last part at center stage.

Once you've sung your last note and your set ends, the audience will applaud. Bow deeply if it feels natural, or thank the audience and nod politely. Put the microphone back on the stand and exit the stage.

This is not the way you *have* to do this. You may feel like doing things another way, and that's great. This is just a solid structure that's easy to remember.

Alternatively, you can simply sing the song with the microphone on the stand if you like. This can work well for ballads.

# Chapter 12
# Singer's Rituals and Secrets to Preserving Your Voice

There are a few things that can help you care for your body and maintain your ability to sing. I'm mentioning the brands that I have had success with, but these are not sponsors, and you may find alternatives that you prefer.

## Traditional Medicinals Throat Coat Tea®

Drinking a warm liquid before or during a performance can be helpful, but it's best to avoid coffee or black tea as the caffeine can be dehydrating. When rehearsing or singing, I always drink a mug of Traditional Medicinals Throat Coat Tea®. It's a strong tasting blend of slippery elm, licorice, and marshmallow root. Don't forget to drink plenty of water too!

## Thayers Sugar-Free Slippery Elm Lozenges®

This is another sweet little helper. Check it out!

## Halls Sugar-Free Cough Drops®

I have used these for a long time. I like the eucalyptus flavor and the cherry flavor.

## How I Cured My Tendency to Catch Colds

I was often sick when I was young. I got colds and the flu more often than most people, I had strep throat, and I even had my eardrum burst when my eustachian tubes became full of fluid.

I had to sing like this for a few weeks and I couldn't even hear myself.

I hate to preach about diet, but I must share with you what I consider to be a revelation. My health improved 100% from adopting the Atkins diet and I hardly ever experience colds or other illnesses anymore. I've been asked by more than one person why I never get sick.

Since I eliminated sugar and starches from my diet, it's as though I have de-aged and that includes my vocal cords. If you get ill often, I suggest trying it. It is also possible to remove a lot of sugars and starches and live a low carb lifestyle without meat, if you are so inclined.

## Secrets to Preserving Your Voice

Please take the following advice to heart: You must preserve your voice at all costs. When you must sing a lot, it's best not to sing every song at full voice. If you are going to be singing a lot of songs, try to alternate some of your more vocally demanding songs with less demanding ones.

Do not try to reach every challenging note on every song. I know you want to sing your best every time, but part of how I've become reliable is not taking chances with my voice on every song, every night. Of course, if you're performing for the Superbowl, this is not the time to hold back!

However, if you are on night one of a six-night gig, as I often was, it may be advantageous to take it easy on your voice today to preserve it for tomorrow, and the next day, and the next day.

## Alternate Material with Other Members

Most of the time when I performed at least one other person sang or played one or more songs. Try to alternate your material with songs being performed by others in your band so that you may have a vocal "rest." Even if you are singing backup in their song, it's not as taxing as being the lead in every song. Try to get one of the other players to sing the lead in a song or play an instrumental version of it, so you can let your vocal cords chill between songs.

If you can, try to look at the set list in advance and share your input. Be sure the songs are arranged in a sequence that is comfortable for you. Try to save your hardest song for the end of the set so that you will be able to rest your voice immediately after. Try not to scream or yell much.

Get the band to have as little dead air between songs as possible, so you to not have to waste your voice on talking between songs. Also, it looks and sounds more professional.

Have the band match your key if the song is not comfortable for you to sing. Having lots of great music to choose from is great for your repertoire, but if your band won't change the key for you to make it comfortable, this can be a problem. Early on I just sang all the songs in their original keys. I didn't even know I could ask them to change the key.

After I started working with professional bands ranging in size from duos to twelve-piece bands, this ceased to be a problem. The more professional the musicians, the more gracious they tend to be about preserving your voice and the more receptive they are to requests for a key change if needed.

## Other Singing Tips

Talk as little as possible between songs and drink plenty of water.

Protect your ears with earplugs. It's hard to do sometimes, but it helps to use earplugs on stage if you are performing with a loud band. Damage to your ears and hearing can happen all too easily in pro music environments. Sometimes it's hard to hear myself with earplugs in, but I still use them most of the time. You don't want to get tinnitus because of damage from loud music.

## Make Sure You Can Hear Yourself in the Monitors

The dedicated speaker called a monitor, which is usually placed on the floor directly in front of you, is there to assist you and make sure you can hear your own voice over the loudness of the instruments around you.

In this kind of environment, before the performance there will usually be a "sound check" where everyone in the band plays or sings a bit so that a good monitor level can be set for whoever is running the sound system for the room or venue you are playing in. Make sure you can hear your voice well enough in the monitor, otherwise you will strain your voice to hear yourself. Don't be afraid to ask for your monitor to be turned up if you are having problems hearing yourself. You might have to ask more than once to have the levels adjusted properly, but this is important. You can lose your voice if you are unable to hear yourself. This is one of the best keys to preserving your voice.

## Get Enough Rest

This may sound silly, like I'm coddling you or giving you obvious advice, but it is hard to perform on stage or in a recording studio if you are ill. Staying warm and hydrated, getting good nutrition, and avoiding illness are much more important to a singer's ability to work than to, say, an accountant or a secretary's work. The accountant can still work even if they can't talk much, but the singer can't work if they can't sing.

# Chapter 13
# Advice from My Mom: Don't Feel Sorry For Yourself

No matter what anyone has told you before, if I were your mom, I would tell you what my mom told me: "You can be anything you want to be."

My husband has a good saying too: "Boldly go!"

Start to believe in yourself fully. Imagine walking into a beautiful art gallery and seeing a painting of exactly what you want your world to look like. Stare at it and step into the painting. Walk so far into that painting that you leave your old self behind.

Don't spend any time criticizing others or being involved in hateful speech or actions. When you feel depressed, think about this. Sometimes as an adolescent when I would feel hurt by something, my mom would say "stop feeling sorry for yourself!"

As my mother had experienced true loss and hardships in her life, this makes me stop and think about how lucky I am and how insignificant most of my problems are. My mother lost a child, my brother, when he was 16. He was killed in a car accident in which he was a passenger. I was only a baby and I can't imagine anyone having to go through that kind of experience.

It must have been so hard for her to move on after the devastation of the loss of my brother. Still, she did move on, and most of the time had a good attitude.

Of course, it's normal to be sad or depressed sometimes, but most of the time, when I examined the cause of my sadness, I was just "feeling sorry for myself."

## Are You "Depressed"?

Sometimes the line between sadness and clinical depression can be blurry, and people can be too quick to medicate. We've all had the idea drummed into our heads via advertisements and public service announcements, but just because someone else has clinical depression, don't assume you do too.

I'm not saying depression is not real. I am saying that even if you are depressed, you may not need to rush to the doctor who may put you on medications that you may not need. I'm not suggesting that doctors are trying to do you harm, but if you go to a doctor for depression, what else do you think they will offer you?

Of course, if you are on medication for depression or any other condition, please do not stop taking them. That might not be safe.

Everyone feels bad sometimes, but do yourself a favor and think about it before voluntarily committing yourself to a life of pharmaceuticals. Think of my mom and her deep sadness. Think of her saying to you, "stop feeling sorry for yourself," and then pick yourself up and move on.

Many drugs can inhibit your creativity as well, so consider that potential consequence before getting on the pharmaceutical train.

Choose to change negative thoughts to thoughts about something you love, like music. Try it a few times; it's not always easy.

Also, look at your sugar intake. It is highly addictive and people get wiggy when they're craving it.

Don't assume you are clinically depressed just because you're sad. Being sad is normal!

It is not my intention to hurt anyone's feelings or suggest that mental illness is not real. I've seen some serious situations up close and I am not dismissing them in any way.

However, it's worth mentioning that it's natural to become depressed if you are not pursuing your dreams. You may be sad and unfulfilled at a job or in a life you don't enjoy. This may be the true cause of your depression. Try jumping into the world of making your dreams come true. You may find that your life becomes so exciting that you forget to be depressed!

# Chapter 14
# Next Steps

I have mentioned how important it is for anyone learning to sing to find a performance outlet in front of others. If you are taking classes from a private teacher, this will most likely present itself to you in the form of recitals.

Quarterly recitals gave my students a reason to try to become the best they could. If you are in school, church, or anything that gives you a chance to sing, try to get involved with their performance programs.

In my early college days, the onstage performance techniques classes helped me transition from singing just a few songs for plays and weddings into being a performer who could sing whole sets on stage. These usually consist of 9 to 12 songs and are a standard length of 45 minutes to an hour.

Having a chance to perform in front of an audience helps you in many ways that you may not realize. When we see an artist we love perform on stage, we tend to forget that it's not just singing they are doing, but also *performing*, which involves the whole body and at least some interaction with the audience.

Handling a microphone, interacting with other musicians, and *performing* can assist you in your singing. If your singing coach has never done any performing, it will be hard for them to help you with it, or even know how important it is. Still, it is necessary for you to learn it if you plan to perform live.

However, you do NOT have to start young to develop musical talent. Think of the now famous Susan Boyle. If Susan Boyle had not had the courage to get up on that stage and audition, she would have never known how far her voice could take her!

Are you an older person who feels like you missed your chance to become a professional, become famous, or even just be heard? You are wrong! Anyone, at any age, can achieve their wildest dreams. The first step is courage.

## How Do You Get There from Here?

Courage is hard! You may find that no one is interested in your dreams to become a paid artist. I had one great person who gave me confidence - my mom. Unfortunately, many families are anything but supportive. You may find that far from a supportive familial environment, you have a bunch of self-proclaimed curmudgeons who can't wait to take the cheapest Seinfeld "nothing" shots at your efforts.

This is a stagnating and stale environment. You may love these people, remember this: **do not cast pearls before swine.** This means do not continually try to share the wonderful gifts God gave you with those who do not have the capacity to appreciate them.

You can still love people who pride themselves on negativity, but for your own good, it might be best not to share your ideas or dreams with them until they have something to offer you besides negativity.

## When Do You Graduate?

Teachers can have a vested interest in keeping you attending their classes for years and years. Sometimes if you're waiting too long for the results you want, and the teacher insists you still need them for improvement, it may be time to move on by yourself.

*"All I can tell you really is if you get to the point where someone is telling you that you are not great or not good enough, just follow your heart and don't let anybody crush your dream."*

- Patti LaBelle, Godmother of soul

## Get Out of Your Own Way

I had a student who was an adult - a retired man. He wanted to learn how to sing and play a specific song on the guitar for an upcoming family function.

I showed him how to do both within a relatively short time - only a few months. However, he didn't understand that he could already sing and play guitar enough to practice by himself at home and perform the song at the family event. We went over the songs again and again and I had gotten him to the stage where he could do it. Despite this, he didn't think he was ready to leave the nest and fly! Is this you?

*"We are educating people out of their creative capacities."*

-Sir Ken Robinson, educational arts advisor

## Stuck in Academia

My mom and I could not afford a university education (although I had won a cash award scholarship from a pageant I was in). Thankfully, I was free to partake in on-the-job training. It was much more beneficial for me to go out and have real-life performing experiences. I doubt that the best universities could have given me the paid opportunities I found for myself.

*"Sometimes getting away from school is the best thing can happen to a great mind."*

-Sir Ken Robinson, educational arts advisor

Do you have a degree you were forced into, either by familial obligations or by yourself because you thought you had to get it? Degrees are great for many things, but don't let education be an obstacle for you. I'm not saying universities are not "a" way, just that they are not "the only" way.

Since I couldn't afford an expensive university, I was able to happily investigate everything I wanted to, without the burden of familial obligations. My mom supported anything I wanted to do.

I love academia and I wholeheartedly respect and appreciate degrees, but I do not believe this is the road everyone can or should take.

In the case of music, for example, it is possible to gain a lot of contacts through your university, but this is still not real-world experience. I could have wasted four to six years of my precious time listening to some expert at a university TALK about music.

I spent targeted time and money only on classes and workshops that interested me. I took a lot of classes but was also flexible so that I could take advantage of opportunities that came up.

If I had been stuck in a four-year or six-year university program, I would have missed a lot of great opportunities and I would have had to wait a lot longer to start working professional gigs - especially the travel opportunities! They were some of the jobs that gave me the confidence and ambition to do more professional jobs. The more I did, the more great musicians I met and the more people called me for singing jobs. They knew I took it seriously and would not let them down. Most importantly, I took myself seriously as someone with a future in music.

## Give Them Extra

Now, in the humblest way possible, I can say that I'm a pretty good singer, but more importantly, I'm reliable. I have gained a reputation for being a high-quality performer who is a "sure thing." I have been called a "secret weapon" by band members because unlike some singers, I could be counted on to deliver the gig to the end. I always gave a good performance and I never lost my voice. This spans a period of many years of on-stage singing, performing, and dancing, three to seven sets per night.

## Learn to Sing in Different Styles and Genres

It is not as important to be a "great singer" as it is to have the ability to sing well and deliver different styles and genres of music. Being able to sing in various styles from country to rock to soul to rap has increased my demand for singing jobs.

This may not be important to you if you are an originals artist performing your own material but widening your scope of music knowledge seldom hurts.

If you want a less expensive alternative to a full degree, I highly advocate checking out your local community college. There are many reasons for this. You can take one class at a time. You can learn a lot of information in a short period of time. The teachers are accredited, unlike many private teachers. There's nothing wrong with private teachers, but I like community colleges too.

It's good to have a deadline for any class or course you attend. I'm not a big believer in sitting back and relaxing in class, pretending to be doing something, because after a while you have learned all you can and there's no reason to be there. It's up to you to know when that is.

## What if You Still Feel You Can't Sing?

If you're ever called upon a stage or a microphone is thrust in your face and you feel obligated to do something but don't feel confident enough to sing, do what William Shatner (best known as captain of the Enterprise) does - spoken word. Speak the lyrics meaningfully as though you are singing them. I encourage you to look up some of the awesome stuff Willie has put out there.

## Bringin' it Home

I've given you almost all I have learned from my experiences as a singer. Now it's up to you.

*Sing Now!*
*Claim Your Right to Express Yourself Through Music.*

# Chapter 15
# Conclusion

So, if I'm so smart, how come I'm not a star?

I **don't want** to be a star!

After spending much of my life thinking that was where I wanted to go, I came to realize that I do not want to be anyone's "idol." I feel insincere asking anyone to "follow me" or to become a member of my fan club or "street team." I feel false acting like I want everyone to watch me and love me and my music, because I have learned that **I don't.**

I want people to like what I do if they like what I do, but I will never coerce anyone into it or try to enslave them into my world by constant tweeting, Facebooking, Instagramming, shading of other artists, etc.

I have discovered that I feel sort of bad when people love what I do because I want to give them something more back - something more that I simply cannot give. I apologize if this sounds bad, but I genuinely do not care if anyone likes what I do or not!

*"It always gave me the creeps when I saw performers who desperately wanted the audience to like them. That's not what I'm about."*

- Barbra Streisand, the diva of divas

# Conclusion

My years of involvement in professional music and working towards a "record deal" revealed to me that I am there for my own appreciation and love for the music. I love performing great songs on stage, both alone and with others, moving around, feeling good, dancing, and most importantly, internalizing those songs. I love getting paid to perform and making a living in music, but I don't need to be a top artist.

I'm here because I love music. Although I can hold my own on stage, I have somewhat of a reclusive personality. I don't feel honest about trying to increase my fan base. They don't have anything to do with my ability to work as a professional singer or composer. I work directly with employers from all over the world and I don't rely on a fan base.

Along with my husband, I own a house on an acreage bordering a river. I would rather spend time in my garden than on social media. Though I'm occasionally called upon to perform live in other places, I choose not to perform in my local town. I simply do not need to be a local star. I like not wearing makeup to the grocery store. There's nothing worse than being recognized while buying toilet paper.

Nowadays, I prefer creating and producing music. I love it when people have positive things to say about the music I've produced for a video game or a film. Ultimately, I'm not on stage anymore, I am behind the scenes.

I am as crazy or even more crazy about music than I was when I was a child with a radio to my ear loving the latest hits, swinging on the swings. I am thankful that I have been able to make my dreams come true by seeking opportunities and assuming that I could be successful.

The End
...but hopefully for you...
The Beginning!

If you've enjoyed reading this book, subscribe* to my mailing list for exclusive content and sneak peeks of my future books.

Visit the link below:
http://eepurl.com/duJ-yf

**OR**

Use the QR Code:

(*Must be 13 years or older to subscribe)

Made in the USA
San Bernardino, CA
26 July 2019